D1411529

DISCARD

Great Artists
Frida Kahlo

ABDO
Publishing Company

Adam G. Klein

visit us at
www.abdopublishing.com

Published by ABDO Publishing Company, 4940 Viking Drive, Edina, Minnesota 55435.
Copyright © 2007 by Abdo Consulting Group, Inc. International copyrights reserved in all
countries. No part of this book may be reproduced in any form without written permission from
the publisher. The Checkerboard Library™ is a trademark and logo of ABDO Publishing
Company.

Printed in the United States.

Cover Photo: Corbis
Interior Photos: Art Resource pp. 5, 13, 21, 27; Bridgeman Art Library 11, 19, 29; Corbis pp. 1, 15,
    17, 22, 26; Getty Images pp. 4, 9, 23; Nickolas Muray/Courtesy George Eastman House p. 25

Frida Kahlo art images pp. 5, 11, 13, 15, 17, 19, 21, 23, 25, 27, 29 © 2005 Banco de México Diego
    Rivera & Frida Kahlo Museums Trust. Av. Cinco de Mayo No. 2, Col. Centro, Del.
    Cuauhtémoc 06059, México, D.F.

Series Coordinator: Megan M. Gunderson
Editors: Megan M. Gunderson, Megan Murphy
Cover Design: Neil Klinepier
Interior Design: Dave Bullen

Library of Congress Cataloging-in-Publication Data

Klein, Adam G., 1976-
  Frida Kahlo / Adam G. Klein.
     p. cm. -- (Great artists)
  Includes index.
  ISBN-10 1-59679-731-2
  ISBN-13 978-1-59679-731-4
  1. Kahlo, Frida--Juvenile literature. 2. Painters--Mexico--Biography--Juvenile literature. I. Kahlo,
Frida. II. Title III. Series: Klein, Adam G., 1976- . Great artists.

  ND259.K33K54 2006
  759.972--dc22
                                                                        2005017888

Contents

Frida Kahlo

Frida Kahlo is one of Mexico's greatest artists. Through her work and life, she helped preserve the Mexican **culture** that she was so proud of. People love her paintings because they capture her electrifying personality. She has been an inspiration to artists of her time and of today.

Kahlo completed about 200 paintings. She was the first Mexican artist to have a painting hung in the Louvre Museum in Paris, France. And, she was the first to sell a painting for more than $1 million. She was also the first Mexican woman artist portrayed on a U.S. postage stamp.

Kahlo lived with many **chronic** problems. Over the course of her life,

Kahlo was featured on postage stamps in Mexico and the United States.

she had about 35 operations. In spite of her illnesses, Kahlo lived with an intense passion. She filled the people around her with hope.

Painting helped Kahlo express the frustrations in her life. Her sensitive, emotional paintings do not hide the life of the artist. Instead, they act as an **autobiography**.

The Louvre bought The Frame *in 1939, after Kahlo's exhibition in France.*

Timeline

1907 ~ On July 6, Frida Kahlo was born in Coyoacán, Mexico.

1910 ~ The Mexican Revolution began.

1914 ~ Kahlo had polio.

1922 ~ Kahlo met Diego Rivera while attending the National Preparatory School in Mexico City.

1925 ~ On September 17, Kahlo was seriously injured in a bus accident.

1929 ~ Kahlo and Rivera married for the first time.

1930 ~ Kahlo and Rivera moved to San Francisco.

1932 ~ Kahlo painted *Self-Portrait on the Border Line Between Mexico and the United States*.

1933 ~ Kahlo painted *My Dress Hangs There*.

1937 ~ Kahlo's work was included in an exhibition at the Galería de Arte.

1939 ~ Kahlo and Rivera divorced; she painted *The Two Fridas*.

1940 ~ On December 8, Kahlo and Rivera remarried.

1943 ~ Kahlo began teaching at La Esmeralda.

1944 ~ Kahlo painted *The Broken Column*.

1953 ~ Kahlo had her first solo show in Mexico; her leg was amputated.

1954 ~ On July 13, Kahlo died in her home, the Blue House.

Fun Facts

- The name *Coyoacán* means "place of coyotes."

- Frida Kahlo told people she was born in 1910. Some people think she did this to associate herself with the Mexican Revolution. Others think she did it so that she did not seem older than her classmates. Kahlo started school late because of the time she spent recovering from polio.

- Kahlo enjoyed spending time with her friends as well as her many pets. These included monkeys, birds, a tiny deer, a cat, and a pack of Mexican dogs called *itzcuintlis*. These animals often appear in her paintings.

Early Days

Magdalena Carmen Frida Kahlo y Calderón was born in Coyoacán, Mexico, on July 6, 1907. She was the third of four daughters born to Guillermo Kahlo and Matilde Calderón y Gonzáles. Frida also had two half sisters from her father's previous marriage.

Frida's father was originally named Wilhelm Kahlo. He was from Germany. He changed his name to Guillermo after he moved to Mexico. Guillermo had a successful career as a photographer for the Mexican government.

Guillermo married Matilde after the death of his first wife. Matilde was a native Mexican of Indian and Spanish ancestry. She was a very devoted Catholic. Her strictness caused trouble for the young, rebellious Frida.

In 1914, Frida suffered an attack of **polio**. She never fully recovered. The disease left her right leg disfigured. She usually hid her leg from others. Still, people at school teased her, and Frida became lonely.

Kahlo helped her father retouch his photographs. This early training affected the way she painted.

The Accident

In 1922, Frida began attending the National Preparatory School in Mexico City. The school had only recently started accepting girls. So, Frida was one of only 35 girls in a school of 2,000 students. There, she began studying to be a doctor.

Frida made friends at the school and joined a group of seven boys and two girls. They were named the *Cachuchas* because of the hats they wore. They would often play pranks on the **muralists** painting their school. The famous artist Diego Rivera was a frequent target of Frida's teasing.

On September 17, 1925, Frida was traveling by bus with her boyfriend, Alejandro Gómez Arias. Sometime during the trip, a trolley struck the bus.

Frida was horribly injured in the accident. She broke many bones, including her collarbone, two ribs, her right leg and foot, and three bones in her spine. She also dislocated her left shoulder.

And, a metal handrail from the bus pierced her **abdomen**. The doctors did not think she had any chance of surviving.

But Frida survived. She spent many months recovering. To cure her boredom and to help her family earn money, Frida began painting. She even painted a self-portrait for Gómez Arias, but he drifted away from her while she was at home healing. Frida was heartbroken.

Kahlo sometimes gave drawings to school friends so they would remember her. In 1926, she painted this self-portrait for Gómez Arias for the same reason.

Diego Rivera

The Mexican Revolution had started in 1910. During the revolution, people overthrew the old government. They fought for equal rights and wrote a new **constitution**. As a result, many people embraced their Mexican **heritage**.

Frida was especially proud of her country's heritage and **culture**. She became devoted to preserving its way of life. Frida was known for dressing in traditional Mexican clothing. This included wearing *Tehuana* dresses from the Tehuantepec region.

Frida was interested in politics and joined the local Young **Communist** League in 1927. And, she reconnected with Diego Rivera. He was more than 20 years older than Frida. But he was attracted to her personality, her politics, and her paintings.

The two decided to marry. However, Frida's parents disapproved. But Frida was in love, so her father gave his permission for the marriage. Frida and Diego married on August 21, 1929.

Rich and Poor

Kahlo wanted her clothing to be an expression of herself, her heritage, and her politics. This idea can be found in her paintings, too. In The Bus (below), clothing helps Kahlo show the contrast between the rich and poor in Mexican society. This work is influenced by Rivera's murals, as well as Kahlo's own political ideas. And, the painting takes after Third-Class Carriage by Honoré Daumier, which is another work about society.

Kahlo painted The Bus *in 1929.*

In America

The **newlyweds** barely had a chance to settle before moving to the United States in November 1930. There, Rivera had an opportunity to paint a **mural** at the San Francisco Stock Exchange. While in San Francisco, Kahlo met Dr. Leo Eloesser. He became her trusted medical adviser.

After Rivera completed the mural in San Francisco, the couple moved to Detroit. There, Kahlo's medical condition worsened. She was pregnant, but the baby died before it was born. Afterward, Kahlo became very depressed. She tried to work through her feelings by expressing them in her art.

Kahlo also missed living in Mexico. She was homesick and wanted to go back. She felt that American **culture** did not fit well with Mexican culture. To express this feeling, she painted *Self-Portrait on the Border Line Between Mexico and the United States* in 1932.

This is not the only piece that reflects Kahlo's feelings about Mexican and American **culture**. When the couple moved to New York in 1933, she painted *My Dress Hangs There*. In the work, Kahlo's *Tehuana* dress hangs amid a detailed scene of New York.

Eventually, Kahlo and Rivera returned to Mexico. They lived in San Angel, near Coyoacán. Kahlo's career continued to be overshadowed by Rivera's. However, she was beginning to gain respect as an artist as well.

Self-Portrait on the Border Line Between Mexico and the United States is a strong example of how Kahlo showed contrasting images in her works. In the painting, the United States is represented as completely industrial. The Mexican side shows growing, living things with natural roots.

A New Home

Kahlo was thrilled to be back in Mexico. Rivera and Kahlo's friend Juan O'Gorman had designed two new houses for them. There was a small blue house for Kahlo, and a larger pink house for Rivera. The houses were connected by a bridge. Kahlo and Rivera could live together, but still have privacy if they wanted.

Although Kahlo was happy to be back home, she and Rivera were having problems. In 1935, Kahlo left Rivera and went back to New York. She returned to Mexico by the end of the year.

Kahlo was a changed person. She was more financially independent from Rivera. And, she was concentrating more seriously on her work as an artist. She created 23 paintings between 1937 and 1938. As always, her paintings are **autobiographical**. Works such as *What the Water Gave Me* reflect the new inner Kahlo coming out.

Opposite page: *In* Memory, *Kahlo's broken heart lies at her feet, revealing her feelings about her troubled marriage.*

Surrealism

In 1937, Kahlo's work was included in an exhibition at the Galería de Arte. This was part of the National Autonomous University of Mexico. She sold four paintings to the famous Hollywood actor Edward G. Robinson in 1938. This was her first major sale.

Poet André Breton came to Mexico in 1938. Breton was an important Surrealist. Kahlo's work impressed him. He thought it should be considered part of the Surrealist movement.

Kahlo had never thought of herself as being a part of a particular art movement. As far as she was concerned, she painted her life. Still, being called a Surrealist would be good for her career. She was invited to participate in exhibitions with other Surrealists.

In November 1938, Kahlo had a show at a gallery in New York. Then, Breton said he had arranged for a showing of her work in Paris, France. But he didn't follow through. In the end it was another artist, Marcel Duchamp, who arranged the showing of 18 of her works.

Artist's Corner

Frida Kahlo

Surrealism is an art movement that focuses on combining unrelated things in unexpected ways. Early in her career, Kahlo was labeled a Surrealist. However, she never considered herself one. She said that she painted reality, not dreams.

Even Kahlo's painting *The Dream (below)* isn't as unrealistic as it seems. She really did have a model skeleton on top of her bed. And she didn't paint a dream, she painted herself dreaming!

Kahlo was influenced by more than just the Surrealist movement. She also included things from Mexican culture, such as combining humans with plants or animals. So despite these outside influences, Kahlo always had her own individual style.

The Two Fridas

Kahlo met many artists in Paris, including Pablo Picasso and Wassily Kandinsky. And, it was at this time that the Louvre bought one of her paintings. But Kahlo hated Paris, and she was delighted to return to Mexico.

Kahlo's reputation was growing. She was being included in more galleries and shows. But soon after her return from France in 1939, Kahlo and Rivera divorced. Even though they loved each other, they had strong personalities that often clashed. The situation made Kahlo very depressed.

During this time, Kahlo completed what is probably her most famous work, *The Two Fridas*. In it, one figure of Kahlo wears a traditional *Tehuana* dress. This shows her Mexican **heritage** from her mother. The other figure wears a Victorian dress, showing her European heritage from her father.

The hearts of the two figures in the painting are connected by blood. One of the Fridas is holding a small portrait of Rivera. Kahlo said that the painting also represents the Frida that Rivera had loved and the one he no longer loved.

The painting shows two Fridas who are connected, yet separate. Kahlo herself was as

In The Two Fridas, *Kahlo painted each figure with its heart on the outside of its body. One heart is broken and represents the Frida that Rivera no longer loved.*

contrasting as *The Two Fridas*. Her paintings can often seem grim. But this was only one side of her life. Kahlo's friends loved her great humor, her concern for others, and her heroism.

Reunion

Kahlo was in pain off and on throughout her entire life. Her health problems were a result of her **polio**, the bus accident, and a spinal problem she had probably had since birth. The pain would not go away.

So, Kahlo traveled to San Francisco again to meet with Dr. Eloesser for medical treatments. During this time, Eloesser worked between Kahlo and Rivera in hope of a reunion. The couple remarried on December 8, 1940.

Kahlo and Rivera returned to Mexico to start their life together again. In the 1940s, they started construction on Anahuacalli, or "the house of idols." It was built as a museum for Rivera's collection

Kahlo and Rivera applied for a marriage license in San Francisco.

of Mexican **artifacts**. Kahlo was devoted to this project that showed such pride in her country's **heritage**.

In 1941, Guillermo Kahlo died. The loss of her father affected Kahlo's delicate health. Her father's photography had influenced her art from an early age. Later, she painted *Portrait of Don Guillermo Kahlo* based on one of his photographs of himself. She **dedicated** the work to her father.

Mexican artifacts, *The Two Fridas, and other works surround Kahlo and Rivera in her studio.*

Los Fridos

Despite her pain, Kahlo worked as much as possible. When she had to stay in bed, she painted using a special **easel**. It allowed her to paint while lying down.

Kahlo was invited to show her work in several galleries, especially in the 1940s. Her new connection with the Surrealist movement influenced her work. But, she always maintained her own distinct style. Many artists respected her opinions, Rivera in particular. Kahlo was setting herself up as a leader in her field.

In 1943, Kahlo was asked to teach at the Education Ministry's School of Fine Arts, La Esmeralda. It was a free school of creative arts in Mexico. Kahlo had never been a teacher, but she fascinated her students.

After it became too difficult for Kahlo to travel to the school, her students came to her home. They formed a group called *Los Fridos*. Kahlo was sad to have never had children of her own. But she found a family in her students.

In Self-Portrait, *Kahlo's eyebrows mirror the hummingbird at her throat. In Mexican culture, these birds were charms for bringing luck in love.*

Broken Column

In the 1940s, Kahlo continued to have more difficulties with her spine and right foot. Her doctor requested that she wear a steel corset to support her spine. Kahlo had a series of operations throughout the decade, but none completely healed her.

Kahlo painted *The Broken Column* in 1944 to show her experiences with her pain. The painting shows Kahlo looking tearful, but brave. Instead of a normal spine, she painted a metal framework in its place. As always, her painting uses straightforward imagery to show her view of her situation.

Despite her health concerns, Kahlo completed several paintings over the next few years. And in 1944, she began her important, colorful diary. But Kahlo's medical conditions worsened. In 1950, she spent a year in the hospital and had seven operations on her spine.

Kahlo in 1944

Autobiography

Kahlo is probably best known for the more than 55 self-portraits she created. In many of her self-portraits, she wears a traditional Mexican dress of the Tehuantepec region and carefully rolls up her hair with fabrics or cords. In these works, Kahlo often exaggerates her dark, nearly connected eyebrows as well as a slight mustache. And, she includes her pets in many of her paintings.

In Self-Portrait with Monkey (below), *the artist and her pet are connected by a red ribbon. The monkey can be seen as a comforting companion. But as a wild animal, it can also be seen as a symbol of the freedom of movement Kahlo felt she never had.*

Rivera slept in the room next to Kahlo's most nights. As much as the couple loved each other, tension remained between them. Still, Rivera tried to cheer her up and entertain her.

Kahlo was loved at the hospital. On days that she could, she put on puppet shows for the hospital employees. Sometimes, she told jokes and teased them. Kahlo was also known for listening carefully to the problems of others. But even so, Kahlo became more and more depressed.

Solo Show

Eventually, Kahlo went back to her home. But she still had to spend most of her time in a bed, in a wheelchair, or in braces. Wanting to thank one of her doctors for all of his good work, Kahlo sent him a painting. It was called *Self-Portrait with the Portrait of Doctor Farill*.

In April 1953, Kahlo had her first solo show in Mexico. It was held at the Galería de Arte Contemporaneo. Her doctors forbid her from attending. But to the delight of the viewers, an ambulance carrying Kahlo arrived during the opening. The artist was carried inside where she greeted visitors and sang ballads in the gallery. Everyone was glad to see her.

In August 1953, Kahlo's right leg had to be **amputated**. She learned to walk on an artificial leg. But her condition worsened. She died in her sleep in the Blue House in Coyoacán on July 13, 1954.

Later in life, Kahlo focused more on painting still lifes. She finished Viva la vida *in 1954, just before she died.*

Kahlo's body was displayed at the Palace of Fine Arts in Mexico City. Hundreds of people came to see her for the last time. She was then cremated, and her ashes were placed in her home.

In 1955, Rivera gave Kahlo's house to the Mexican people to be used as a museum. Today, the Museo Frida Kahlo is one of the most visited museums in Mexico.

Glossary

abdomen - the part of the body located between the chest and the legs.

amputate - to remove, especially to cut a limb from a body.

artifact - a useful object made by human skill a long time ago.

autobiography - a story of a person's life that is written by himself or herself.

chronic - when something is always present or occurs for a long time.

communism - a social and economic system in which everything is owned by the government and given to the people as needed.

constitution - the laws that govern a country.

culture - the customs, arts, and tools of a nation or people at a certain time.

dedicate - to give a message showing affection or thanks in an album, book, or other artistic work.

easel - a stand that holds a painter's canvas.

heritage - the handing down of something from one generation to the next.

mural - a picture painted on a wall or ceiling. A muralist is a person who creates such a work.

newlywed - a person who just married.

polio - the common name for poliomyelitis, a disease that sometimes leaves people paralyzed. It usually affects children.

Saying It

Coyoacán - kawih-oh-ah-KAHN
Guillermo Kahlo - geel-YEHR-moh KAH-loh
Louvre - LOO-vruh
Marcel Duchamp - mawr-sehl doo-shahn
Tehuantepec - tay-WAHN-tah-pehk
Wassily Kandinsky - vuhs-YEEL-yuhih kuhn-DYEEN-skuhih

Web Sites

To learn more about Frida Kahlo, visit ABDO Publishing Company on the World Wide Web at **www.abdopub.com**. Web sites about Kahlo are featured on our Book Links page. These links are routinely monitored and updated to provide the most current information available.

Index